OVERCOMING SHYNESS:

Break Out of Your Shell and Express Your True Self

by

Erik Myers

D1416601

DISCLAIMER

This book has been written to provide information to help you overcome shyness. Every effort has been made to make this information as complete and accurate as possible. However, there may be mistakes in typography or content. The purpose of this book is to educate. The author does not warrant that the information contained in this book is fully complete and shall not be responsible for any errors or omissions. The author shall have neither liability nor responsibility to any person or entity with respect to any loss or damage caused or alleged to be caused directly or indirectly by this book.

Editor: Wayne Purdin
Photography by: Megan Hildebrand
Cover Design: Alerrandre from FIVERR

DOWNLOAD THE AUDIOBOOK FREE!

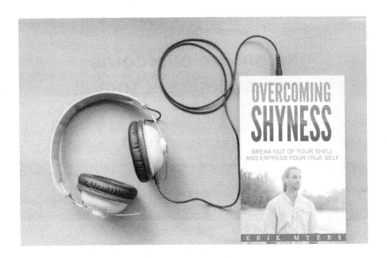

READ THIS FIRST

To express my gratitude for downloading the book, I would like to give you the audiobook version 100% FREE!

CLICK HERE TO DOWNLOAD
(Or go to: www.overcomingshyness.co/audiobook)

Before we overcome shyness, let's get social!

I'd love to hear from you and learn more about your story. If we're not already connected, send me a request and message!

Instagram @ErikMyers4
Facebook.com/ErikMyers4
YouTube: Myers Mindset
Erik@overcomingshyness.co

DEDICATION

This book would not have been possible without the love and support from my beautiful wife Dominique, my mom (aka Mama Sharr), my siblings (Kelsey, Ryan, & Carrie), my mother-in-law (Mama Laborte), and every friend who believed in me before I believed in myself.

This book is in loving memory of my dad,
Craig Gilpin Myers

Table of Contents

INTRODUCTION

Have you ever had that experience when you knew the answer to a question asked in a class or had a great idea in a meeting at work, but no matter how much you wanted to raise your hand and speak out, there was just something holding you back?

Or maybe you're minding your own business walking down a hallway or busy street and see from afar someone you barely know. You see them but they haven't seen you yet, and suddenly you activate your inner James Bond as you strategically reroute your path to avoid an awkward conversation.

What about when you're introduced to a friend of a friend and you have absolutely no idea what you're going to say after "Hi, nice to meet you"? So you look back to your friend with a desperate expression on your face that screams *"HELP ME!"*

You definitely aren't alone, my friend.

These experiences weren't just occasional things for me while growing up; they were part of my daily routine. I actually became so good at being shy and hiding in my little shell that I "earned" the title of *Most Quiet* during my senior year of high school. Yay?

Those awkward social scenarios that I referred to weren't just uncomfortable; they were *painful.*

My stomach would tighten up and I would literally exhaust myself by overanalyzing and critiquing everything that I did or said. Since those feelings and thoughts were a daily occurrence, I rationalized in my head that this was just who I was and how it was going to be.

Ultimately, my shyness grew into social anxiety. Combine those anxious thoughts with insecurities and the death of a loved one, and I was one step away from ending my life during my second year of college. (I'll explain more on how that all happened in the second chapter).

But you and I both know that this book isn't about me; it's about you and your future.

I want to share with you the exact steps I've taken throughout this journey to help you overcome shyness, improve social skills, and (most importantly) express more of your *True Self*.

Whether you're an introvert or extrovert, loud or quiet, reserved or open, it doesn't matter. The principles and path I'm going to lay out in this book will help you stand apart from the crowd, make more friends, and feel more comfortable in your own skin!

What are we waiting for? Let's get started! First, you need to know....

WHAT TO EXPECT

The first half of the book will be your chance to go within and begin to strengthen your mindset by understanding what's been holding you back, how to create lasting change, and start focusing on your exciting new future.

During this section, I'll be opening up and sharing with you my own journey and then explaining each principle and how it can be applied to your life.

I do this to demonstrate that these aren't simply theories that I've read about or researched. I've lived them, and I know they have the power to have the same benefits for you.

The second half of the book is when it starts to get REALLY exciting. I'll be sharing with you the best techniques and practices that you can use out in the real world to build your "confidence muscle" and start applying these practical social skills.

I'll refer to these as your *Back Pocket Tips* because you can pull them out anytime, anywhere. You can use them to spark up and enjoy a friendly conversation and potentially make a new friend.

When you use one of these techniques, you may notice a little confidence boost and pep to your step afterwards. Embrace it.

Other times, it might feel awkward and uncomfortable (especially at first) and that is completely normal. Embrace it.

There's one more thing you should know before we dive both feet into this journey together.

Throughout the book, I'll often refer to you and your *True Self*.

The opposite, of course, is your *False Self*. I believe that you and I are behaving as our *False Self* whenever we believe in the thoughts that make us feel anxious, fearful, judgmental, lonely, stressed, worried, or in constant need of validation.

Our *True Self* is when we are aligned with the thoughts that make us feel worthy, loved, accepted, thankful, relaxed, connected, honest, forgiving, trusting, or at peace.

Your *True Self* is not a reference to any religious practice but, rather, a state of mind in which you feel *good* and connected with the core of what makes you human.

Now that you're warmed up and stretched out, let's start with....

SECTION 1:

MINDSET

Chapter 1:

THE FOUR-LETTER F WORD

Fear. "The greatest prison people live in is the fear of what other people think." —David Icke

Many people form opinions about what they know nothing about, including you and me, but act like they're authorities on the subject. So why should we fear other people's opinions and comments? I spent years being afraid of talking to other people out of fear of their disapproval.

But I eventually discovered that most people weren't judging and critiquing me as much as I thought they were, and those who did really didn't know me. I was trapped in my own mind because of FEAR.

Before I discovered how to cope with my fear of talking to another person, I had two (very) different strategies to relieve anxiety and forget my insecurities in social situations.

One of them was really effective. The other one led me to almost end my life.

Whoa!

The first strategy worked really well and came natural to me as a kid: playing sports. Swimming was my favorite (maybe because there's no obligation to start a conversation, since everyone's head is under water most of the time), and I actually became pretty good at it.

If I wasn't in the pool, I was kicking a soccer ball around, shooting hoops, or playing baseball. As long as I was moving and active, I was good to go.

Which makes sense, right? It's tough to stay in your head and let fear get the best of you when you also have to dodge a ball or guard an opponent at the same time. I'd be totally emerged in the game or race and didn't have time to worry.

Once high school (and organized sports) ended, I had to find a new outlet for my shyness. I was too afraid to pursue my dream of becoming a college athlete so I did what I thought was the next best thing.... I went to the sports-crazed University of Oregon!

By this time, my shyness was slowly transforming into social anxiety. I skipped the dorm experience (so many people...that sounded terrifying!) and lived with my small group of really close friends from high school.

The good news was that I found a new way to escape my fears and be myself. The bad news was that it wasn't exactly the best type of outlet.

I did what I thought every college kid was doing: drinking and partying as much as possible. Although I was barely passing my classes at the time, I was succeeding...in the art of Beer Pong and King's Cup.

Don't get me wrong. I don't think it's horrible to let loose and have a few drinks. It's just that for me at that time, it was solely about escaping the *crappy* thoughts that were consuming my mind.

Drinking wasn't a healthy strategy, but it was an effective one to get out of my head. It was the only time I felt like I could be myself.

In class or at work, I was really reserved and detached from the world around me, but after a few (too many) shots with my buddies, I would come out of my shell and finally give myself permission to...well, be myself and talk with people.

This perpetual cycle of living in constant fear and binge drinking took me down a dark path, which I'll talk more about in the next chapter.

Right now, we need to know where our fears come from and how we can begin to see them for what they really are.

Why Fear and Shyness Get Along So Well

Fear has become so embedded in our nervous systems because thousands of years ago (I'm talking caveman days) it was an extremely important and useful emotional response. It was our internal warning sign that would protect us from the saber-toothed tigers that were trying to make our ancestors their dinner.

In the modern world, we still have that same emotional trigger in our bodies, it's just that we aren't being hunted by a hungry beast. Most of our social fears stem from the caveman days.

Back then, if you were rejected and shunned by the tribe, it was a death sentence. You either died of starvation or the elements, or you became some predator's meal.

We no longer live in tribes and depend on them for physical survival. Unfortunately, we're still hardwired to belong to a group and fear rejection. These fears are totally irrational. Today, if someone rejects us, nothing happens. We're totally safe. We know this logically, but our brains are still hardwired to equate rejection with death.

Rejection doesn't feel nice, but that's not enough to cause paralyzing fear. This is our brain's way of keeping us safe from something it perceives to be a real threat to our survival because it's still operating in caveman mode.

In most scenarios (for quiet people like you and me), fear of rejection comes up when we're meeting someone new, giving a speech in public, being interviewed for a job, or maybe even simply answering a phone call.

It's important to understand that fear isn't something external. We can't pick it up, pack it tight, lock it in a box, and throw away the key in efforts to get rid of it. It comes from within.

It's even more important to realize that because you're a quiet or shy person, you probably have a very powerful imagination.

Our active imaginations can serve us either as our best friends or

9

our worst enemies. We can use it to create a highlight reel of all the times we felt awkward and uncomfortable around other people, or we can envision ourselves meeting someone new and boldly shaking their hand, looking them in the eye, and making an amazing first impression.

So how do we effectively channel that adrenaline and racing heartbeat when fear is triggered in our minds?

We've got to make an internal shift from...

Camera In, Camera Out

One of my favorite classes later in college was (go figure) an introduction to acting. It was *way* outside of my comfort zone.

The professor was an exuberant man and he taught us with immersion, not just boring lectures talking about theories and history.

Within the first week of the class, he had us do an exercise that I'll never forget.

One by one, he challenged us to stand up in the front of the class and give two 1-minute presentations sharing our backgrounds and a little bit about ourselves.

The first time each person got up, he gave him or her a mirror that reflected the person's face for the full minute.

I'm not sure who felt more uncomfortable each time someone did this: the presenter or the audience.

When it was my turn and I started talking with a giant mirror reflecting back at me, I could only notice how my hair was messed up, the food that was stuck in between my teeth, and the weird way my lips were shaped as I spoke.

The second time around, there was no mirror. As you can imagine, the energy in the room was completely different this time. Each presenter was much more smooth and everyone was way more comfortable.

After everyone had presented twice, he went on to explain that when a mirror is in front of us (either real or imagined) we're only focused on ourselves. We predominantly think about how we look and how others perceive us. We're critical and judgmental. As a result, our camera is IN and we are much less effective as communicators.

When we flip the camera around, however, we have the ability to focus all of our attention and energy on people and our environment.

Once our camera is OUT, we are free to connect with the world around us.

Do you go throughout your daily routine with your camera IN or OUT? Are you trapped in your head or are you living in the present moment?

While someone else is talking, are you thinking about what you're going to say next?

It's okay if you do this. It doesn't make you crazy, it means you're human and you have room to grow.

The very first step is to start becoming aware of where you decide to focus.

Remember, when our camera is IN, we're consumed with fear. When our camera is OUT, we're able to tap into our....

Chapter 2:

POTENTIAL

As I mentioned in the last chapter, I was heading down a dark path at a fast rate. One particular morning I'll never forget. It was after another night of excessive drinking, and as soon as I woke up, I knew that something was wrong.

As I replayed back in my mind everything I could remember from the night before, I started feeling dumb...really dumb. *Why did I say that? Why did I do that? You're such an idiot, Erik!*

I got out of bed to get some water and see if any of my friends were awake. I needed a distraction.

No one was up yet and our apartment looked like the scene from *The Hangover;* all that was missing was a tiger in the bathroom and a missing tooth.

I paced up and down the halls and one word kept screaming in my head over and over again: *discontent, discontent, discontent!*

The regret that I was feeling (combined with a massive hangover) was too much to take, so I stepped outside for some fresh air and started walking.

It was a crisp, chilly day in Eugene, Oregon. I was in my own little world and I kept dwelling on a very scary thought: I was losing control of my actions and I was losing control of my life.

Before I knew it, I was at the infamous *Autzen Footbridge,* hunched on the rail, and staring down at the river passing below. I'm not sure how long I was there but it felt like hours as I just watched the water go by.

What if I just jumped off and let my body go?

Was that the alcohol talking or did I really just think that? I had never contemplated a thought like this before, and it didn't sound like a horrible idea. I was desperate for anything that would quiet the garbage that was going on in my head.

Once I came to my senses and realized how ridiculous that was, I got away from the bridge before I did something stupid.

But the contemplation of that thought scared the shit out of me. I knew something *had* to change; otherwise, I'd be back at that bridge before I knew it.

A couple of weeks later, I (accidentally) started reading a self-help book. I didn't know it was one of *those* books, and if I did, I don't think I would have read it.

How I was introduced to this book is a little embarrassing, and if you judge me for this, I won't hold it against you.

On Thursday nights, my roommates and I would get a bottle of cheap rum and watch the newest episode of MTV's *The Jersey Shore*. We fed off the energy of the show in our attempt to live the Gym, Tan, Laundry lifestyle.

At the end of an episode, one of the characters, Vinny Guadagnino, came on the screen and talked about his latest book about anxiety, *Control the Crazy.*

Before I knew it, I was on *Amazon* downloading the book, which was weird because I *hated* reading. But this one was different and I couldn't put it down.

I don't think my head stopped nodding up and down like a bobblehead as I scrolled through each page. As I learned about his story and internal battles, it occurred to me: *maybe I'm not the only one who feels isolated and disconnected from the world.*

If this guy, who had become a TV celebrity and best-selling author, experienced the same negative thoughts, self-doubt, and insecurities that I was feeling, then there *HAD* to be others like me as well.

A Shift in Perspective

In the book, Vinny talked about how each person has around 60,000 thoughts per day. SIXTY THOUSAND! That blew me away. And then it scared me. I estimated that at least 75% of my thoughts consisted of:

Why am I so shy?
There's something wrong with me.
I shouldn't have said that.
Someday, I'll....
Why am I so awkward?
I should have said something!
I wish I were more confident.
If only I were like....

Then something *clicked*. If Vinny had those same negative thoughts about his anxiety and he changed, why couldn't I change? I just had to do what he did. This began to strengthen a belief in me that what's possible for one is possible for all.

So I started meditating, lifting weights, doing yoga, journaling what I was thankful for, eating healthier, reading more books like this, and (most importantly) I sought out counseling.

During this process, there would be times when I would envision what my life would be like once my shyness was no longer in the driver seat. I would see myself being social, and it felt incredible to imagine that freedom.

I was also slowly becoming obsessed with this idea of *personal development*. Reading a book for a class about biology or chemistry bored me to tears. But if I picked up a book that taught me how to control my emotions and strengthen my mindset, I couldn't put it down.

I began to believe (for the first time) that I really could reprogram my mind. I started to think of my brain like a computer. There were inputs and outputs that just needed to be adjusted.

Although I was starting to feel better on the inside, from the outside, my life didn't look much different. I didn't feel comfortable telling many people about these new little tricks I'd

14

been picking up, but I could feel a shift starting to build up. I had no idea that the biggest turning point of my life was just around the corner (and we'll explore it in Chapter 3).

Why aren't I living to my fullest potential?

I think we both can agree that every human has the same amount of potential. We all may have grown up in different parts of the world with different families that raised us and received different educations, **but** with a functioning brain and a heart that still beats, we all have the ability to become whatever we put our minds to.

So why do some people continue to have more, give more, and become more while others have a tough time keeping their heads above water and constantly struggle? Why do some people exude confidence while others feel more and more awkward as the days go by?

The answer became clear when I first heard Tony Robbins talk about what he calls his "success cycle," which states that Potential leads to Action, which produces Results, which reinforce Beliefs. Take a look:

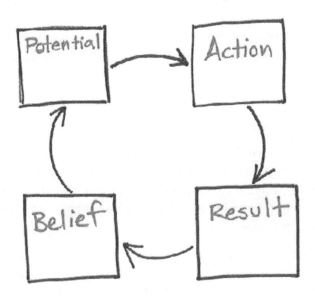

This cycle can be used in any area of our lives to either build us up or tear us down. Before I had my breakthrough, which I'll talk about in the next chapter, I was using this cycle in a *very* unsuccessful way with my shyness. Here's what it looked like for me:

Potential: I would remind myself daily that since I had always been a shy and reserved person, I would always be like that. I was born that way; it's genetic, and there's nothing I can do. That's just the way it was.

Action: I rarely introduced myself or tried to make new friends. I would sit near the back of the class and pray that I wouldn't be noticed, and I chose the shifts at work where I would be isolated with the least amount of interaction as possible.

Result: I would get extremely uncomfortable and wouldn't know what to say in daily conversations.

Belief: My brain would say, *See! I told you you're awkward and shy.*

Wash, rinse, repeat. That would strengthen my belief and fear so I'd live out my own self-fulfilling prophecy. Having this belief was detrimental to my growth. Because I believed I was inherently shy, I rarely bothered trying to change it. And when I did try to overcome my shyness and it didn't work, that just confirmed my belief that something was inherently wrong with me or was a genetic fault in my brain.

What's the solution?

As much as I wish I could, it's simply not possible for me to give you more potential, make you take more action, give you better results, and strengthen your belief in yourself. Luckily, the obstacle that's been holding you back from expressing your *True Self* is also your opportunity.

I shared with you my story of hitting rock bottom at the beginning of this chapter because it's in moments like that, when we decide *enough is ENOUGH,* that we actually start to make change.

It would be great if we could sit around and wait until the day came that suddenly we magically developed a "confidence muscle" and were instantly more comfortable around people. But you and I both know that life isn't like that.

The answers to all of your problems already live within you; you just need to bring them to the surface.

Using Your Imagination for All the Right Reasons

Whether you realize it or not, your mind is constantly envisioning (and creating) what your future is going to be.

What you and I are going to do together is to start replacing more positive images than negative ones in your mind's highlight reel. We must become certain in our mind about who we are becoming long before it actually happens.

Have you heard the story of Roger Bannister?

Before 1954, no one had ever run a mile in less than four minutes. It was believed by most that the task was simply **impossible**. Up until that year, the fastest time recorded was 4:01, and the general consensus was that the human body wasn't designed to run any faster than that.

The difference between Roger and the rest of the world was that he was **certain** that he could do it and would imagine himself crossing that finish line in less than four minutes.

His opportunity came on May 6th, 1954 when he finished with the time of 3:59:4 and became the first man to ever break the four-minute barrier.

The amazing part about this story is that 46 days later, another man broke the four-minute mark, and since that day, thousands of people have run a four-minute mile (including many high school athletes).

I'm not asking you to run a mile in less than four minutes. Nor am I suggesting you become a reality TV celebrity or professional public speaker.

What I'm asking (and challenging) you to do is to be open to the idea of believing in your potential of what's possible by visualizing

17

yourself as the person you want to become.

Several scientific studies have proven the positive benefits of visualization. Dr. Maxwell Maltz stated that if a person's imagination is vivid and detailed enough, it tricks their nervous system into thinking that what they visualize is actually real. If, every day, you give yourself (at least) 5-10 minutes to visualize yourself being the confident person you want to become, it will become easier for you to act that way in public.

When you visualize, you're drafting a blueprint of the person you want to become. You're experiencing what it feels like to act confidently in a social situation. Then, when it actually happens, it's easier because you've already rehearsed the scenario in your mind and know what it feels like. This is how you can prepare for a social event because you've already done it in your mind and visualized it going well.

Many other people believed in me before I believed in myself, and now I'm asking you to make room for the person you want to become, and you will have your....

Chapter 3:

BREAKTHROUGH!

Six months had gone by after reading *Control the Crazy,* and my life looked...pretty much the same.

I was feeling a little better from the healthy new habits I was developing. I had cut back on the drinking and was more focused on my classes. Yet, despite these subtle changes, I was still scared to talk to people.

I had no idea I was about to experience my first major breakthrough in life.

The spring semester was coming to an end, and my roommates had decided to go home for the summer to work. Since I had failed a handful of classes that year, I didn't have a choice other than staying in town to play catch up and continue working at the campus Recreation Center.

With my best friends gone and the apartment to myself, I *had* to make some friends or I was going to spend the next three months with my good buddies, Netflix and Xbox.

Then *it happened.*

It was a day just like any other. I was handing out towels and locks to the guests and then for some strange reason and in an instant, I experienced a *jolt* of energy that rushed through my body. I started initiating conversations with my co-workers and the afternoon gym-goers.

I was smiling, laughing, asking questions, giving compliments, and making new friends. It was EXHILARATING!

But where the hell was this coming from?

I didn't give myself enough time to ponder that question (like I would have usually done) and went with the flow.

The next four hours flew by, and my shift was coming to an end, but I didn't want this to stop. I was having more fun than I had had in a LONG time.

By the time I got home and had a chance to reflect, I was feeling like Bradley Cooper's character (Eddie Morra) in the movie *Limitless*, minus the magic pill. I experienced a natural "high" from in-depth conversations and I knew my life would never be the same. I was hooked.

The rest of that summer was truly transformative. Each new day, new person, and new conversation was an opportunity to learn and challenge my fear. I began making new friends at work and in my classes. These were people who I saw almost every day but was always too afraid to go beyond small talk with.

I started going to parties and having fun without drinking too much alcohol (what a concept!) and went on adventures around the city of Eugene. I was open to anything and everything but felt most alive from simply enjoying long, honest conversations with new friends.

For the first time, I was excited about going to work and class. The story in my mind was slowly shifting from *"I'm so awkward and weird and will always be shy"* to *"I've got nothing to lose! Life is too short to hide in my little shell, and I actually really enjoy talking to people!"*

I started to believe that maybe, just maybe, I could overcome this shyness that had held me back for so long. My dad was a people person and I had always wanted to be more like him in that way, and this was the first time that I started to think that it was possible.

New questions started entering my mind each day that I had never thought of before such as "What else am I afraid of?" I rationalized that if I could conquer *this* fear of opening up and talking, I could do anything. I started to bring those fears to the surface and went after them one by one. All of my self-constructed obstacles started to become opportunities.

As I mentioned before, I had always wanted to be a college athlete. The problem was that I quit the sport I was good at (swimming) when I was 12-years-old to pursue basketball. I loved basketball; I just wasn't very good at it. Most colleges aren't interested in an undersized, unskilled kid who played JV for three years and then rode the bench his senior year.

But I knew I was a good swimmer, and with this newfound belief that anything is possible, I became extremely curious as to what it would take to earn a spot on a college team. This dream was starting to take hold of me and I couldn't shake it off.

You and Your Breakthrough

By now, I hope you're thinking, *Okay, this is all great, Erik... but how am I going to overcome my shyness?*

Whether it's overcoming shyness, expressing more of your true self, improving your social skills, or (literally) any other area of your life, a breakthrough is what will take your life to the next level.

One more thing before we dissect how to create your breakthrough. I said it before and I'll say it again: this book is about taking ACTION! Otherwise, you'll continue to bounce around from book to book, seminar to seminar, opportunity to opportunity, always looking for an answer when the answer is already inside of you.

Let's bring it to life.

What exactly is a breakthrough?

A breakthrough is the moment you declare, *"I can never go back to who I was,"* and you begin to embrace your new path.

Chances are good that you've already experienced at least one major breakthrough in your life. Maybe it was when you decided you'd never smoke another cigarette or eat fast food. Maybe it was when you forgave someone you'd been holding a grudge against for years. Whatever it was, something *shifted* in you, and your life will never be the same.

Understand the Power (and Limitations) of Your Story

We all have a story circulating in our minds about who we are and what we're capable of. To have a voice in your mind doesn't make you crazy; it makes you human. That story that you carry with yourself each day is shaping your perception of the world.

I can (and will) give you strategies and techniques to come out of your shell and become a confident communicator, but if the story in the back of your mind keeps repeating, *"Yeah, but this just isn't for me; it may work for others but not for me."* Then you'll remain stuck until you change your story.

The difference between those who are social, outgoing, and confident in everyday conversations compared to those who feel timid, insecure, and reserved simply comes down to the thoughts that each person believes in with absolute certainty.

What's the story that's perpetuating in your mind? Is it empowering you or does it bring you down? Does it give you energy or make you want to hide? If your best friend talked to you the way that you talk to yourself, would you still want to be their friend?

As I shared earlier, the never-ending thoughts in my mind at that time were: *I'm shy and awkward, people think I'm weird, and I'd better not speak up and make a fool of myself!* Whether these thoughts were true or not was completely up to me, so I was living my self-fulfilling prophecy.

To change the story in my mind, I started practicing a technique that I had learned from meditation. I would observe my thoughts as if they were clouds passing through my head. If the cloud made me feel good, I would let it stick around. If it didn't feel good, I would let it float on by and out my ear.

We become the thoughts that we consistently focus on and attach our emotions to.

Instead of repeating in your mind, *I just don't want to be shy anymore!* I'm challenging you to focus on what you want, not what you don't want. When that thought-cloud that says, *I'm a social person and it's easy for me to make friends* sneaks into your mind, make space for it and let it hang out for a while.

Wait! Isn't this that classic BS "positive thinking" crap?

No, my friend, this is psychology.

Energize Your Thoughts

Just like the stories that shape our perception, our daily energy level (or state of mind) creates how we interpret the world around us.

It's difficult to act confident and strike up a conversation if you're feeling timid and afraid. You'll psyche yourself out before you even have a chance.

Think about your mind as if it were a thermostat. Let's say that over the years, you've found that you feel comfortable setting your thermostat at 72 degrees. Now, every day, good things happen that make your internal temperature rise up and bad things will happen that cause a drop in temperature. But you always find a way back to your comfortable, laid-back 72 degrees.

To overcome your shyness with higher energy when talking to people, you're going to need to manually reset your thermostat to 75 degrees. That will take effort. Your mind isn't going to like this because that's not what it's habitually used to, and it will feel uncomfortable at first.

Guess what? YOU control your thermostat. It doesn't control you.

How do we control our energy level? With our bodies. **Positive emotion is created by motion**. All of the latest research will agree that we can change our biochemistry and physiology by movement.

Don't get me wrong; I'm not suggesting that you start doing squats before you shake someone's hand and start a conversation (unless that's your thing).

I'm suggesting that you start creating daily habits that get your body moving and put you in a heightened state of mind each day.

You and I both know that trying to talk ourselves into doing something just doesn't work. We've got to move the body and energize our thoughts.

The goal is to become aware of when your energy level starts to drop and find your strategy to bring it back up on a daily, moment-to-moment basis.

Putting It All Together

Your breakthrough *will* come when you have a heightened state of mind with a new exciting story that you believe in.

Remember what we talked about at the beginning of this chapter: it happens in a moment. The cool part is that you get to decide when that moment happens. It can literally occur as soon as you put this book down or it can happen a year from now when you finally give yourself permission to change. The decision is up to you, and as you do, you'll start....

Chapter 4.

EXPANDING YOUR IDENTITY

We've talked a lot so far about all these *changes* that you're either seeking, experiencing, or will be experiencing soon in the pursuit of overcoming your shyness. Let's not forget that *change* is inevitable no matter what. What we're really after is growth and expansion to become more of your *True Self.*

I don't think there's anything wrong with you in the first place and I don't want you to trick yourself into believing that there is. This journey isn't about you *changing* your identity; it's about *expanding* your identity.

This is about bringing out the social, playful, passionate person that you are, and that requires digging past the fears, discovering your potential, and experiencing your breakthrough to get there.

My Leap of Faith

As that unforgettable summer was coming to an end, I knew it was time to start making some new plans. For the first time (in a long time), I had the courage to dream about what I *truly* wanted.

I didn't have all the answers, but I was sure of these three things:

- I wanted to live somewhere warm.

- I wanted to become a college swimmer.

- I wanted to start my own adventure.

With a whole lot of enthusiasm and determination, it wasn't long until I found my answer. I decided it was time to leave my nest and comfort zone in Oregon and transfer down to a small school in sunny Southern California. It was the same school that my older sister graduated from (so it wasn't completely random) and I was ready for a fresh start.

Transfer deadlines were approaching and I didn't exactly have the extra thousands of dollars for tuition, but in my mind, it didn't matter. I would do whatever it took to make it happen.

It's amazing how fast you can overcome your fear of talking to someone on the phone or asking for help when your dreams become bigger than your fears.

One month later, my car was packed and I was ready to go.

The Freedom to Be Myself

Bliss.

Pure bliss and liberation circulated through my body as I made the two-day road trip toward my new life. I hadn't felt that free and relaxed since I was a kid.

I remember thinking on the drive, *I can be whoever I want to be. No one there knows who I've been. This is INCREDIBLE!*

Have you ever had that feeling?

It's empowering and exciting to know that you can create a new life for yourself at *any* time. It doesn't require transferring schools or moving to somewhere new, all we need to do is make the decision and commit.

As I settled into my dorm and got situated, I didn't waste any time getting involved with my new community. This urgency was partly fueled by fear. I was more afraid of *not* making new friends than of being rejected.

Within the first two weeks, I earned a spot on the swim team, joined student government, and got a job working at the front desk in a dorm. For all three of these activities, I had one primary motive: make friends and have fun.

I acted as if I had been a social person my whole life, and for the first time, it was easy and happened effortlessly.

I was only able to stay at that school for one semester (so it was really more like a study abroad) because I wasn't able to get enough loans or scholarships to cover the expenses, but I will always cherish those three months as some of the most vital towards my growth as a person.

I developed lifelong friendships, became a college athlete, and faced fears on a daily basis. I was content.

The biggest surprise from that experience was a passion that I never knew I had and I doubt I ever would have realized it if I hadn't tried new things and expanded outside of my comfort zone.

If you want to become more confident and achieve your goals in life, sooner or later, you're going to have to get out of your comfort zone and put yourself in situations where you can potentially be rejected but from which you will always grow and learn.

Robert Allen, author of *One Minute Millionaire,* wrote, "Everything you want in your life is just outside your comfort zone."

Getting out of your comfort zone is when the real magic happens in your life. Yes, it can be painful and uncomfortable at times, but it's like getting into a cold shower. When you finally take the plunge, the water stings for a few seconds, but then you get used to it and actually start to like it. Then afterwards, you feel awake and refreshed.

It's exactly the same with trying new things, getting out of your comfort zone, and expanding your identity.

During one of our weekly Monday night meetings, the student body president asked me to share my story and give a little pep talk each week. She was going to call it *Motivational Mondays with Erik,* and, to be honest, it scared the living daylight out of me.

So, of course, since it scared me and was way outside my comfort zone, I decided to give it a go.

That Monday night, as I opened up and shared what had led me to move down to California, I felt my spirit come to life and I was absolutely energized by the challenge. That night, I discovered my passion for inspiring others through stories.

Before that night, if you had told me that I was going to become a public speaker, I would have called you crazy and checked you into a mental hospital for treatment.

Maybe you already know what you're most passionate about or what your life's calling is. Or maybe you feel like you're looping in circles with no direction or purpose.

If you believe your shyness has been holding you back, then it's time for us to get to work. Let's dig deeper to bring out more of your *True Self*.

Bringing Out the Best of YOU!

Since your goal here is to no longer be shy, then we need to start thinking about what your life will be like when you're confident. I believe that you have talents, insight, and skills within you that you aren't even aware of yet.

The main way that you're going to bring your uniqueness to life is by setting exciting goals and heading in a new direction.

If all we can think about is overcoming shyness, we'll stay trapped in that lower level of energy and fail to rise up to the next level. Once we start to focus on more of what we want, our brain begins to find the answers for us.

My whole life started to change, and I discovered confidence in my social skills once I began to follow (and trust) my heart, and I'm absolutely certain that the same can happen for you once you decide to follow yours.

Goal Setting That Doesn't Suck

You're going to enjoy the end of this chapter because I'm giving you permission to DREAM like you used to dream when you were a kid.

It's very important to go through this exercise with a "no-limits" attitude. Think in terms of what you *really* want, not merely what you believe is *possible*. Inspired ideas and actions derive from inspiring dreams, so dream big and don't hold back.

You're going to have a lot of fun with this, but before you start, make sure you're in a GREAT state of mind (not a *good* state, not an average state, but you should be nearly bouncing off the walls because you're so excited). Start doing some jumping jacks or do a little dance, whatever it takes!

Now grab a pen and your journal and find some space where you can be by yourself, and play some light music in the background if you think that would help.

- **Become clear on what you want:** Set a timer for 30 minutes. Make a list of 50 goals you have for your life: long-term goals, short-term goals, personal goals, family goals, health goals, spiritual goals, business/career goals, financial goals, social goals, hobby goals, and everything in between.

Since our objective with this book is to overcome any shyness that's been holding us back, it's important to include the goal of the new social/confident/peaceful person that you intend to become, but don't limit yourself there. Don't hold back and don't stop until the 30 minutes has ended. If you have more than 50, no problem! Make sure you have at least 50. If not, take more time.

- **Your top five:** From those 50 goals, choose five of them that are the most exciting to you. That's how you know you've got the right ones. At least one of them should be reflective of the social, confident person that you're becoming during this journey. Once you've chosen your five, find images that represent what that goal looks like to you.

- **Make it real:** Now we're going to bring those images to life and print them out. You can either make a vision board or use notecards (or both!) and strategically place these cards or board in locations where you'll see them every day.

- **Attach affirmations:** For each goal, you're going to write down an affirmation as if the goal has already happened. You may be thinking, *isn't this that hocus-pocus positive thinking crap?* No, it's psychology. The more specific you can be about **exactly** what you want and when you want it, the better the chances your brain can provide those answers. Effective affirmations are positive statements, charged with feeling, written in present tense first person, beginning with "I am...." For example, "I am a confident, vibrant person who loves to socialize!"

- **See, feel, and believe them every day:** The purpose of setting goals isn't for the attainment of the goal itself. It's who you must become in the process in order to be worthy of the desired outcome. What we're doing to our subconscious mind when we look at each image, affirm it (with certainty), and feel it in our body is creating the emotion and belief we associate with that goal, which strengthens the magnetic force within you and guides you where you need to be. The reason why affirmations don't work for many people is that they fail to create the energy associated with the goal. Don't be a boring adult while you affirm these statements. Read (or say them out loud if you can) with ENERGY, passion, and joy. Place the notecards or vision board near your bed so you look at the images and read the images first thing in the morning and right before you go to sleep.

You might be wondering, *Why am I setting goals? I thought this was about overcoming my shyness.* Great question. In the same way that the smoker can't stop smoking until he creates a new habit, you won't be able to overcome your shyness unless you're focused on projects or goals that you'll be too excited about to be scared or shy.

I know this sounds strange, but I've experienced it in my own life, and if I can do it, I **know** for certain that you can do it too.

Once you've set your goals and have them placed where you'll see (and **feel**) them every day, it's time for you to...

Chapter 5:

GET REAL AND MOVE ON

This is your personal checkpoint.

Before we continue further and start taking the action that will create long-term and lasting change with your *Back Pocket Tips*, we must assess where we are and get real with ourselves.

Remember, I didn't experience a breakthrough and start the process of overcoming my shyness until months after journaling, reading new books, and seeking out professional help from a counselor.

I won't ever forget how free I felt after each counseling session I had. At the time, I didn't feel comfortable sharing what I said in my counseling sessions with my girlfriend, close friends, or even my family. I needed to express my true emotions and thoughts to someone who didn't know me; otherwise, I would have held back.

I'm giving you permission right here, right now, to let it all out.

How to Let It Out!

These are two of the best methods (from my experience) to express yourself so you can move forward: professional counseling or writing your thoughts out in a journal.

If you don't yet feel comfortable talking to someone about what's *really* going on inside of you, write it out! It's free and the benefits can be just as effective.

Set a timer for 30 minutes and simply write whatever comes to your mind. Don't hold back and don't stop writing. Make sure to do this with pen and paper rather than digitally. Start doing this every day (or at least three times per week) to build up a momentum.

Journaling is one of the most important tools to get real with yourself because it forces you to collect your thoughts, impressions, dreams, experiences, and feelings; organize them; clarify them; and express them in a way that often results in profound insights that can change your way of thinking and acting. It contains descriptions of events as well as reflections about the events.

Journal writing is the easiest type of writing because it doesn't involve anyone but yourself; you're the only reader. So you don't have to worry about grammar, punctuation, logic, and content. You can write whatever is on your mind and heart without any hesitancy because you won't be offending anyone or embarrassing yourself. You can really let the creative juices flow.

The journal becomes your map to self-discovery. In the hectic pace of modern life, it gives you an opportunity to stop and reflect on the meaning of events and circumstances in your life. It engages you in a conversation with yourself about important issues in your life. Together, these strengthen your identity and your ability to process life experiences in a positive manner.

The rules of keeping a journal can be distilled down to three simple principles:

- Date each entry. At the time you write, it doesn't matter if you add the date, but when you look back over your journal, it helps to keep things in perspective.

- Write when and how you want. Draw out your feelings at times to give journaling variety and interest. Also, if you force yourself to write, the writing will become dry. It's better to take a break with writing than force yourself to write when you don't want to.

- Always tell the truth. Why bother to write if you aren't going to be honest with yourself?

The following tips can help you gain a momentum on keeping a journal: You can write at a specific time every day, preferably when you know you won't be disturbed. And you can write a specific amount (pages or minutes). The important thing is, write every day until you've let it all out!

If you're ready to talk to a counselor, seek out local professionals. If you're still in school, chances are you have access to someone like this for free or at a low rate. The bonus to talking to someone like this is that they'll listen *and* be able to offer solutions to guide you in the right direction.

We're coming to the end of the first half of the book, which has been all about mindset so far. Before we move on to the second half, in which you'll learn about the *Back Pocket Tips* and start harnessing their power, we need to discuss a truth that can be hard to face....

Chapter 6:

WHO YOU SPEND TIME WITH IS WHO YOU BECOME

Remember when we were younger and our parents, teachers, and coaches would warn us and say, "I don't think it's good for you to be spending so much time with *so-and-so;* he (or she) is a bad influence on you." If you were like me, you probably ignored their advice and hung out with that person anyway.

Well, it turns out they were on to something. Personal development guru, Jim Rohn famously said, "You become like the five people you spend the most time with. Choose carefully."

Have you been choosing carefully lately?

Either those five people are stretching and challenging you to become a social and confident person, or their complacency and shyness is rubbing off on you. Whether you like it or not, you're always being influenced by the people whom you choose to spend time with.

I'm not saying that it's completely *their* responsibility because you're the one who decided to spend time with them. They're behaving in the best way that they know how.

People change, and friends come and go. You don't have to stay friends with people who are constantly putting you down and keeping you stuck in bad habits and negative thinking. Take a look at your current friends, relatives, and role models and ask yourself if these people are good for you. If not, limit the amount of time you spend with them.

I love my buddies from college and still keep in touch with them to this day. But at that time, I knew I wouldn't be able to keep up with that lifestyle for very long before I'd find myself back at the bridge. Ultimately, that meant I had to distance myself from them for a while, and that was **tough**.

Like I said, this change isn't as easy to do as some of the other strategies we'll talk about later. I'm not suggesting that you start completely cutting people out of your life, but it's important to start becoming aware of the people you spend time with, and make the conscious effort to surround yourself with those who will influence you to become who you want to be. Hang out with people with the same goals as you, who will be supportive and nonjudgmental.

How do others influence us?

Because of our human desire to connect and bond, we adopt the philosophy, habits, attitudes, standards, and lifestyle of those around us.

We like people who are like us, right?

If most of your friends believe that people are scary and social situations are awkward, it's no surprise that you (most likely) will think this way too.

On the other hand, however, what if you had the type of friends who loved meeting new people and diving deep into conversations?

How would you think differently? Which of your beliefs would change? How would you perceive others on a daily basis?

This was a huge shift for me. I had always been afraid to speak up or introduce myself because I believed that others would judge me (probably because I was constantly judging myself) but when I started spending more time with social people, I learned that people aren't that scary at all.

By observing my extroverted friends spark up conversations, I saw how good it made others feel to be recognized. Most of us walk around each day with an invisible sign around our necks that says, "Notice me!!! Make me feel important or special." Social people naturally use the *Camera Out* technique and it's become a habit for them to start and engage in conversations.

Surrounding yourself with social people is so powerful because you adapt to their level of consciousness. It doesn't take a lot of willpower since you're subconsciously picking up their patterns and behavior.

Find Mentors and Role Models

Like I mentioned, you don't want to simply start cutting off those people from your life who you don't believe are contributing to your growth. Everyone has something special about them, and you have the power to bring that uniqueness out of them.

You will need to make the conscious effort to start surrounding yourself with mentors and role models who exemplify the characteristics that you want. There are two types that you want to connect with: direct and indirect mentors.

Direct mentors are the people you already know who possess the skills and attitudes that you want to adopt. These could be a leader at your job, a coach, a teacher, a community leader, or even a peer or friend.

If you're having a tough time thinking of people like this near you, don't worry! We live in the greatest time in human history for connecting with like-minded people, and at the end of this chapter, I'll show you how to find them instantly.

Indirect mentors are people you aspire to become like and have a lot of respect for. It doesn't matter if this person is dead or alive, or lives close to you or in another country. It could be a professional athlete, artist, author, speaker, philanthropist, entrepreneur, or anyone else. There are no limits here.

I believe that I became so hooked on reading and listening to audios from successful people after reading *Control the Crazy* because it felt like we were sitting in the same room next to each other and he or she was giving me all of their secrets. I didn't have to go out and learn all of life's lessons through my own experiences; I could learn from them.

You have the same opportunity.

Join Our Community

There is strength in community that can help you overcome problems that would be insurmountable on your own. Look at the success of 12-step programs and group therapy. To overcome shyness, it is essential to find a community of people who have the same goals as you and understand how you feel. These people do exist and they're looking forward to meeting you on Facebook. I invite you to come and join our online community. In the process of writing this book, I also created the Overcoming Shyness Community group on Facebook. I encourage you to request to join that group (www.facebook.com/groups/overcomingshyness) and get plugged in!

In here, we share videos, articles, and ideas to help each other out. More importantly, it's a chance to meet other people who can relate and want to connect. This is "positive peer pressure" at its finest. All that's missing right now is...YOU!

See you in the group!

SECTION 2:

YOUR BACK POCKET TIPS

Chapter 7:

THE POWER OF YOUR PEARLY WHITES

We made it! The first section of the book can be difficult because it requires us to take a good, hard look at ourselves in the mirror, and it's not always easy to see what's really going on.

Now I'm going to share with you the exact tips and strategies you can use out in the real world to break free and conquer your shyness once and for all. These aren't just theories, these are trial-tested tactics and proven through my own (and many others') experiences.

Think about this time that you spend each day reading and learning as your practice, as if you were playing a sport.

When you're not reading, it's game time! You get to put these strategies to work and try them out. You may make some mistakes, but that's okay. Be open and patient with yourself and trust that, with practice and persistence, you'll continue to improve.

We're focused on progress, not perfection.

Now let's lace up and buckle down, we've got work to do.

From Super Shy to Smiles for Miles

One of my first classes when I got down to my new school in Southern California was Spanish 102 at 8:00 in the morning, four days a week.

Most college students aren't too thrilled about learning a new language, let alone right after the sun has risen. I was no exception.

But I was also still in the "honeymoon" phase of overcoming my shyness and a crazy idea came to me during the first week.

On the five-minute walk from my dorm to the class, I would typically pass by 15-25 people. One morning, for whatever reason, I decided that I would simply smile at each person I walked by.

You can imagine the thoughts that popped up in my mind the first couple of days I would do this.

You look like such a fool! Stop smiling, you idiot! People are going to think you're SO weird!

Whenever those thoughts would arise, I reminded myself of the ideas I had been learning from *Control the Crazy*. I would shift my focus back to my breath and look for the next person I could share a smile with.

To my surprise, 99% of the people would smile back. That gave me the satisfaction that *maybe*, even just for a moment, I had the power to help make someone's day a little better.

After a couple weeks of my new smiling routine, I was ready to take this challenge to the next level. I started to add a *Good morning!* to each passing student or professor.

Again, it blew my mind what a positive response I would get back from people.

You might be thinking, *Well, duh, Erik! Of course, people would respond this way.*

Well, here's where this new little habit became transformative for me. By the time I would get to that Spanish class after my five-minute fear-crushing walk, I would feel *really good*. For the first time (in...ever!), I was raising my hand in class, making friends, and not hiding in the back of the room!

Conquering my fear started with a smile. Yes, a simple smile. And here's how it can do the same for you.

The Science of a Smile

As oversimplistic and elementary as this first strategy is, it has the power to boost your confidence instantly and research will back this up.

You can find hundreds of studies that provide evidence for the benefits of smiling (even when you don't feel like it!) but, to me, it comes down to this simple truth: we can't feel good *and* bad at the same time. It's just not possible.

Elan Sunstar, author of *Smile: Secrets of the Healing Power of Your Smile,* wrote, "Your mental and emotional state is affected by the state of your body, and vice-versa. So, if you make a change in one, you make a change in the other because there is a mind-body-spirit continuum.

Smiling breaks your pattern of negative thoughts and forces your brain to start searching for memories, ideas, and events that make you feel good."

We can't expect to confidently talk to people if we don't feel *good* on the inside.

Up until this point, I would guess that you associate pain and uncomfortable feelings with talking to people. It's only human nature for us to avoid pain and increase pleasure. It's easier to remain quiet and keep our thoughts to ourselves.

Remember when we talked about creating your breakthrough? We agreed that you would need to change your state of mind. Nothing will change your state faster than smiling, even if you need to force it at first!

The Cold, Chilly Truth

I'll let you in on a little secret. I'm one of those crazy people who wake up way too early, not because I have to, but because I like to. It's an extremely empowering feeling to take control of my thoughts and my mind first thing in the morning.

No matter how long I've been doing this, I *never* feel like getting out of my warm cozy bed at 4:00 AM, but I've conditioned my brain to do it by the *3...2...1* strategy that we'll talk about in

43

Chapter 11.

After I do my zombie walk over to the bathroom, the first thing I do is brush my teeth and jump into a cold shower. (Yes, you read that correctly.)

Right before the freezing cold water splashes on my face, I force a great big smile. I probably look like a crazy person, but it moves me into action. After the initial shock wears off and I'm able to catch my breath, I feel amazing. It's not as crazy as a polar bear club member plunging into ice-cold water, and it has similar health benefits such as improved circulation, decreased depression, healthier skin and hair, strengthened immune system, increased testosterone, increased fertility, and greater energy and well-being. However, if you have high blood pressure, it's not advisable to take cold showers, as they constrict blood vessels.

In the same way, I take a social plunge. When I'm in a social situation where I know I could potentially become fearful and anxious, I make the conscious effort to start smiling.

Instantly, my stress is reduced, and I'm able to stay in the moment (instead of being trapped in my mind) to keep my camera *out* and engaged *in* the conversation.

You might think, *Well, yeah, but I don't want to be a phony person by faking smiles for the rest of my life.* Touché. But I'm willing to bet that after forcing a smile on your face for 5 seconds, it won't be fake anymore. You'll actually start to feel better and it will transform into a real smile.

You'll start to give off a different type of energy when you walk around with a smile. Not only will *you* feel good but you'll start to make others feel good too. Win-win!

Your Vibe Attracts Your Tribe

As you start to smile more, you'll notice that other people will begin initiating conversations with you more often because they'll be attracted to your good vibes and become curious about what makes you so happy.

Although this is something that might have terrified us before, now we've got nothing to fear. In Chapter 10, I'll give you the most practical advice for what to say when you get to that point.

Carrying on through your day with a smile lets people know that you're safe. Instinctively, people want to protect themselves. Without words your smile says to others, *Hey, it's okay! I'm safe. I'm not out to hurt you.*

Before I started consistently practicing this smiling strategy, out of fear, I would walk with low energy and very little expression on my face.

As a result, I was left alone, and I liked it that way because I believed that hiding in my little shell was easier than facing my fear and opening up to others.

We can try to convince ourselves that we're happier by isolating ourselves from others and avoiding vulnerability, but it's just not the truth. We'll begin to connect with more people and experience life in a much more rich and meaningful way when we smile and allow ourselves to be seen.

Practice, Practice, Practice

As silly as this sounds, you're going to need to practice your smiling on a daily basis. If you're not sure where to begin without feeling like an absolute fool, start by practicing around your home.

Smile while you're washing the dishes, smile while you're making coffee, smile while you're in the shower, smile while you do your laundry, and everything else. As often as possible, SMILE!

And don't just use the muscles around your mouth to give a half-hearted smile. There are hundreds of muscles in the face. Use them all. Smile so big that you make the corners of your eyes crinkle.

If you live with your spouse, family, or roommates, they undoubtedly will think you're a crazy person at first. That's okay. Let them borrow this book and encourage them to take a few minutes to read this chapter so they understand why you're doing it.

Once you're ready to take it to the next level, mindfully begin smiling when you go outside to walk your dog, get the mail, take out the trash, and everything else.

Finally, start this smiling practice when you're at work, at school, on the bus, waiting in line at a restaurant, and everything else.

This will feel awkward at first. Please remember this simple fact of life: others aren't thinking about (and judging) you as much as you think they are. Most people are too preoccupied with their own lives to be thinking about you. When I realized this, I was set free from my mind, and you can experience this liberation too.

If your mind starts to give you every reason why you shouldn't practice smiling, thank it for its concern about your safety, then give yourself permission to feel the incredible sensations of a big smile and start to....

Chapter 8:

BE AWARE OF YOUR BODY LANGUAGE

Similar to the "smile muscles" that you're practicing and developing, your second *Back Pocket Tip* is your body language.

Here's good news for people like you and me: 55% of communication is through our nonverbal cues, 38% is our vocal inflection, leaving just 7% for the actual words we speak.

If you're like me, at time, you get worried that the words you speak are going to come out the wrong way. Knowing those percentages took away that pressure of getting the words right, so all I had to do was focus on improving my body language.

I'm going to teach you a simple and easy-to-remember technique that you can use anytime you're in any social setting, and your confident body language will actually make you feel more confident.

Are you ready? You don't want to miss this one.

As Easy as ABC!

You're going to love these ABCs because you will see an immediate difference in the energy you bring to any conversation. It will work if you're meeting someone for the first time, talking to your boss or professor, with a group of friends, or anything else! All you need to remember is ABCDE, which stands for:

A: Adjust your shoulders

B: Breathe deeply and release
C: Clasp your hands
D: Display your SMILE!
E: Eye contact

I can't count how many times ABCDE has saved me in a potentially uncomfortable social situation. Whenever my nerves start to rattle and my heart starts racing, I resort back to this powerful strategy.

It only takes about ten seconds to make the adjustment as you go through the sequence. Let's break down each of these. Sound good?

Adjust Your Shoulders

Allowing our shoulders to drop forward and slouched over gives the perception to others that we lack confidence, decisiveness, and even sincerity.

Now, I know you're a sincere person, but your body language might suggest something different. The answer is simple. All you need to do is stand up straight, pull your shoulders back, and open your chest. No need to go all Superman or Wonder Woman with this one, just a subtle shift of the shoulders.

Let me be honest with you; I've had an extremely tough time staying true to this habit.

My wife, Dominique, is constantly reminding me to stand up straight and stop slouching. At first, this really bothered me. The male-ego can be a pain in the ass for everyone at times. But she was absolutely right (rule number one of marriage: she's always right) and her reminders have helped me to make progress.

If your posture needs some work, I would suggest asking your partner, friend, or coworker to call you out every time you're slouching. It will make all the difference in the long run.

Breathe Deep and Release the Tension and Worry

Now that your shoulders are pulled back and your chest is open, take a deep breath, hold for 4 seconds, exhale in a long sigh, then repeat one more time! When you exhale, imagine that all the tension in your body and worry in your mind are being expelled.

If you're all tight and tensed up, the person you're talking to will subconsciously recognize those cues and know that you're feeling uncomfortable.

Taking two deep breaths will begin to calm your nerves and help you return to the present moment so you can stay focused on the person and conversation.

Clasp Your Hands

Do you ever feel like Will Farrell's character (Ricky Bobby) from Talladega Nights and finding yourself thinking, *I'm not sure what to do with my hands*? I do. A simple adjustment in the positioning of your hands can make all the difference.

One of the most common mindless habits we have when talking to someone is that we become all fidgety with our hands.

While talking, do you ever touch your face, eyes, or hair? Do you ever adjust your clothes or jewelry?

Again, the person you're talking to will subconsciously recognize those cues and know that you're feeling uncomfortable.

Although this part of the sequence is called "Clasp Your Hands," there are a couple of different options you can choose from. However, as a general rule of thumb, I would recommend keeping your hands up by your chest when speaking, and down by your lap when listening.

As far as the positioning of your hands goes, you can either have them clasped together or in steeple pose where your fingertips are touching. I prefer the steeple because I think it gives off more a calm and collected vibe, but, ultimately, it's up to you!

Display Your Smile!

This one is self-explanatory. When listening to others speak, make the conscious effort to give a simple smile and nod accordingly. You want the person to feel that you're not just listening but you're also engaged and interested. Put a smile on yourself to feel good and help others feel good.

Eye Contact

If you're like me and feel intimidated by the idea of looking at someone directly in the eyes in a conversation, I've got good news for you! You don't have to...at first. I'll explain what I mean by that in a moment.

It's important to remember that in a conversation, the person you're talking to knows and feels that you're genuinely interested in what they're saying, and the quickest way to gain this trust is through eye contact.

During my freshman year of high school, I remember one of my teachers instructing us on how to make eye contact. He suggested looking at the person's nose, lips, or in between their eyebrows until you feel comfortable making direct contact.

This is a great place to start until you've built up the courage to connect with their eyes. And once you do, don't feel that you have to maintain eye contact. You can go back to nose contact any time you feel uncomfortable.

Now that you're smiling and exuding confident body language, you're in a great position to practice....

Chapter 9:

THE 3-FOOT RULE

With more than half the battle won by mastering your body language, it's time to utilize some of the *Back Pocket Tips* that will help you actually start, you know, talking to people!

Chances are that if you're like me, you've become *really* good at avoiding conversations and hiding in your shell. I've got exciting news. It's going to be **a lot** easier to start (and carry on) conversations than you thought.

In no time, you can become a brilliant conversationalist with these simple, powerful techniques.

The first trick to start carrying in your back pocket is the 3-Foot Rule. In simplistic terms, this means that you'll make the conscious effort to spark up a conversation with anyone within about three feet of you.

If you've been shy for most of your life, I know what you're thinking: this sounds scary. It's okay to have that thought, but I want to encourage you to keep an open mind.

Plus, I'm going to show you how this is going to be much more simple than you think.

The Danger of NOT Talking to Strangers

If your parents were like mine when you were a kid, they reminded you not to talk to strangers. This was great advice when we were young and naive, but we're not little kids anymore.

In fact, if we don't talk to strangers (who are all really just one conversation away from becoming a good friend) then we'll go through life struggling with our career, relationships, and overall happiness.

One of our basic human needs is connection with others and the world around us. Trust me, I know how lonely and empty it feels when you don't have that connection, and I want to help you communicate your *True Self* more effectively.

But what am I going to say?!

The majority of us don't talk to people we don't (yet) know because we're afraid of what they might think of us and/or we don't think we would know what to say.

I'd bet that either just now as you've been reading this or sometime in your life, you've thought about talking with someone but then instantly froze up as you tried to structure an opening sentence. I'm guilty of doing this so many times.

I'm going to share with you a simple process that will guide you to executing the 3-Foot Rule.

The Four Magic Words

Are you ready to hear the absolute best and proven opening line to start a conversation?

"Hey! How are you?"

WHAT?! That's it?!

Yep. It's okay to be mad at me for how simple this is, but research backs it up. This is great news if you're worried about coming up with the perfect opening line.

I learned this trick from Vanessa Van Edwards, who is a Behavioral Investigator for the Science of People. My wife and I saw her keynote speech while at a conference in Nashville.

During her talk she said, "This opening line is easy and effective. Don't drive yourself crazy coming up with something clever or witty. This has worked for me 100% of the time."

Those four words have stuck with me ever since and we saw a huge difference when we starting applying this to our 3-Foot Rule.

Once you get the conversation started, you'll want to make sure to...

Shake Their Hand

This isn't just custom or protocol; there's a science behind it. As soon as your hands meet, both of you will release oxytocin in your bodies that will strengthen your bond.

We won't dive too far into the handshake (though I would encourage you to Google or YouTube it) but for the sake of simplicity, remember to keep your hands dry and your grip firm, neither too soft nor too aggressive.

Introduce Yourself

I like to keep my introduction as short and simple as possible, so I can keep the conversation focused on the other person and learn about them.

If I were at the gym, I might say, "Hey, how's it going? I'm Erik; what type of workout are you doing today?"

If I were standing in line for coffee I might say, "Good morning, how are you? I'm Erik; what's your go-to cup of coffee?"

Once they respond, you can continue to ask more questions (we have a whole chapter coming up soon to talk about the power of questions).

You'll instinctively know when the best time is to shake their hand and introduce yourself, so don't get caught up in saying the right words (remember it's only 7% of communication) and following the process in a specific order.

It's more important to simply get the conversation started than to say the perfect opening line.

Now that you've broken the ice and done the toughest part of the 3-Foot Rule, there are a couple of tricks you can keep up your sleeve to keep the discussion flowing smoothly.

Smile and Nod

These two techniques are lifesavers for my fellow introverts and me. We tend to freak ourselves out before a conversation has even started because we think we need to know exactly what to say. That's not true at all.

My goal in every conversation is to effectively execute the 80/20 rule. I want the keep the other person talking for 80 percent of the time while I only speak for 20 percent.

Why? Because, let's be honest, most people like to talk about themselves. Now, I didn't say we like opening up and talking that much with strangers, but when we feel comfortable, we love to give our opinions and share our thoughts.

This is something we can use to our advantage in any conversation. While the other person is talking, gracefully smile and nod. Research has proved that this will keep your fellow conversationalist talking.

Frank Bettger once said, "I no longer worry about being a brilliant conversationalist. I simply try to be a good listener. I notice that people who do that are usually welcome wherever they go."

Use your listening skills to your advantage and you'll experience incredible conversations wherever you go.

Closing the Convo

As you sense the conversation to be ending soon, you want to ask the other person something about their future. It doesn't need to be a deep question; it can be as simple as:

"What are you up to the rest of the day?"

"What are your plans for the weekend?"

The purpose of this is to set yourself up for a smooth ending. As you shake their hand to say goodbye, you can say:

"It was great chatting with you, Tom; have a good time hiking with your family this weekend!"

The last impression can be just as important as the first one. It reminds the other person that you truly care and you really were interested. It leaves you both with a good feeling about the interaction.

If the other person abruptly ends the conversation, don't take it personally. Maybe they want to connect with other people in the room, have an appointment to keep, or just have to use the restroom. Remember to smile and tell them it was nice talking with them.

You might be wondering, *what if I want to keep in touch and stay connected with them?*

Great question.

The most effective strategy I've discovered is asking if he or she is on Facebook. I ask this for two reasons.

The first reason is because, at the time I'm writing this, there are 1.79 billion users on Facebook, so the chances are good that they are.

The second reason is because I doubt I would ever text or call this person out of the blue. That comes off a little creepy to me and could potentially send mixed signals, especially if the person I met were a woman.

If they're on Facebook and want to connect on there, I always let them type in their name (it's faster that way) and, again, it strengthens the trust and bond between us since most of us cherish our phone as if it keeps us on life support.

Don't worry if they don't have a Facebook account or they don't want to stay connected. That rarely happens, and even if it does, you can still be thankful for the conversation and opportunity to strengthen your "confidence muscle."

You can now successfully execute the 3-Foot Rule anytime, anywhere. Don't feel obligated to do it *all the time*, but I want to challenge you to start doing it once a day (or even just once a week at first).

Once you've done the toughest part and initiated the conversation, you're going to need to know how to....

Chapter 10:

ASK (GOOD) QUESTIONS

If you only take away one good *Back Pocket Tip* from this book, then this is the one you want to highlight, underline, and start implementing IMMEDIATELY!

Remember how earlier I mentioned that you want to keep the other person talking for 80% of the interaction and you'll become a brilliant conversationalist? This is how you do it...

Ask questions!

I learned the power of this technique the day I had my breakthrough and my whole life began to change. I started to become very curious about what exactly I was afraid of.

Since my biggest fear was other people and remaining calm in a conversation, I started asking other people as many questions as I could think of.

What you'll begin to discover is that you'll learn a lot from other people and a lot about yourself.

The ultimate outcome from asking questions is finding common ground with the person you're speaking with. Many of us feel shy and isolated because we don't believe that other people can relate to what we're feeling.

News flash: we all have *something* in common.

Generally speaking, we all want to feel loved, we all have our fears, we all want to feel accepted, and we all want more out of at least one area of our life.

With enough digging and sincere curiosity, we can connect with any given person from anywhere in the world. Your purpose for asking questions in a conversation is to find that connection and build upon it.

The Power of a Question

When my wife and I moved out to Maui, I started working as a barista at a nearby coffee shop located inside of a resort in Kaanapali.

No matter how crazy the morning rush was, I did my best (some days were tougher than others) to ask a question or give a compliment that might make that customer's day just a little bit better.

One day, a man in his early thirties walked in for his morning espresso with his three young boys who were running and jumping in every which direction. His face held the expression of exhaustion from trying to keep up with his kids but also genuine joy and love for them.

While handing him his double Americano, I asked, "What's the best part about being a father?"

He was completely thrown off and looked puzzled by the question. He stopped and pondered for a good five seconds before answering, "Their unconditional love. It's the type of love that can't be put into words."

He gently smiled as he started to walk away before he stopped mid-stride, turned back to the counter, and put a $20 bill in the tip jar.

I'll never forget the way his face lit up after answering the question.

The tip he left was extremely generous. But what was far more valuable was the lesson he taught me.

We all have the power to make another person feel noticed, grateful, or appreciated by asking the right question.

What Types of Questions Should I Ask?

The depth of your questions will depend on your relationship with the other person.

You might not want to ask someone, "what's the purpose of your life?" the first time you meet them (or maybe you do!) and on the flip side, you probably don't want to be asking the person you've been dating for three years, "what do you like to do for fun?" or something like that.

Here are some of my favorite questions to ask someone I'm still getting to know:

What are you passionate about?
What's your family like?
Who is your favorite historical figure?
What's your story?
What's the best part about being a parent?
If you could have lunch with anyone, dead or alive, who would it be and why?
If money were no object, how would you really spend each day?
If you could visit anywhere in the world, where would you go and why?
Have you read a book that completely changed your perspective?

These types of questions go beyond the surface level and give you the chance to learn more about a person's *True Self* without making them feel uncomfortable.

If those questions seem a little too much for you, scale it down and start with the basics:

What do you do for a living?
Where did you go to school?
Where did you grow up?
Where's your favorite place to eat?
What's your favorite movie?
Who's your best friend?
What's the best vacation you've ever been on?

Again, it's less important *exactly* what you're saying and more important that you're engaged in the conversation and continuously asking questions that stimulate the other person's mind.

Just keep asking questions and then comment on what the other person says. That's all you need to do in a good conversation. And if an awkward silence threatens to put an untimely end to the conversation, have some ready-to-go questions to fill it.

Be an Active Listener

What most people do while the other person is talking is think about what they're going to say next. If you have a habit of doing this, make the decision *right now* that you're going to work on quieting your mind and being fully present and actively listen while the other person speaks.

The five elements of active listening are:

- Provide positive feedback both verbally and nonverbally. Verbal feedback can be "I see," "yeah," "gotcha," etc. Nonverbal feedback includes looking them in the eyes, smiling, and giving appropriate facial expressions and gestures.

- Ask questions to clarify what you're hearing. If you're not sure about the meaning of a speaker's words, ask clarifying questions such as "What do you mean by that?" Be sure the speaker understands your intentions are to seek clarification rather than to challenge.

- Reword what the speaker is saying to see if you understand them correctly. Preface your rewording with such comments as: "So, if I understand you correctly, you're saying…(state what you think they said in your own words) …Is that right?"

- Avoid interrupting. Keep silent except for verbal feedback or asking a clarifying question until they're completely finished. Then give your responses, ignoring any emotional argument they may have used and focusing only on facts and logic.

- Be open-minded and tolerant and express neither agreement nor disagreement. In your role as a listener, it's more important to clearly understand the speaker than to indicate whether or not you agree or disagree with them. That way, you can usually get more of the truth behind their words. Once you know their truth, you can come to some understanding.

What you'll discover as you begin to practice this is that you learn a lot more about a person by the emotion behind their words, rather than just their words alone.

Start paying attention to the other person's body language. If you notice the emotion doesn't align with the words they speak, start asking more questions about it.

Have you ever watched the show *Criminal Minds*? It's a guilty pleasure for Dominique and me. We love the psychology behind it and the way the profilers observe people's behavior.

We don't have to work for the Behavioral Analysis Unit of the FBI to use this technique to start noticing the truth behind people's words. As we keep our *Camera Out,* we'll be given clues on what type of questions to ask next.

We can't get better at this skill simply by reading a book; we've got to put this *Back Pocket Tip* into everyday use!

The next time you're out in public, ask at least one person a question. Notice your surroundings, find common ground, and spark up a conversation.

It's okay if the interaction is short and doesn't go anywhere, this is more about you developing these new skills and facing your fears.

To put this all together and ensure sustainable success with your communication skills, you're going to need....

Chapter 11:

THE SECRET SAUCE

There's a very good chance that you've already heard many of the ideas and techniques you're reading about. Sometimes, we simply need to hear it from a different perspective and from someone else's story.

I've given you the blueprint to get in the right mindset and the *Back Pocket Tips* that have been proven by hundreds of thousands of people to overcome shyness and improve social skills.

This last technique is an idea you may not have heard of before, and I believe it is the secret sauce to *actually* make this all work for you.

How many times have you known *what* to do and even *how* to do it but you still didn't follow through?

How often have you had an idea of what you could say to spark a conversation with someone who looks interested but you held back and hid in your shell instead?

Your days of self-sabotage end...now.

How to Stop Screwing Yourself Over

That was the title of a TED talk that popped up on the Suggested Videos (Thanks YouTube?) and out of pure curiosity, I clicked on the link. I was totally unaware that I was about to stumble upon life-changing information.

In the video, Mel Robbins introduces what she calls "The 5 Second

Rule" (not the one about picking up food off the ground and eating it within five seconds).

She suggests that we all already know what we want but knowing is not enough. It's just not as simple as Nike's "Just Do It" slogan; otherwise, we'd all be living the life of our dreams.

The reason we don't is because when our feelings and our thoughts are up against each other in the moment of decision, our feelings always win.

Sound familiar?

I really want to make new friends in class; I just don't have the courage to introduce myself.
I really want to speak up in our weekly meetings at work; I just don't feel like it.
I really want to ask that girl out on a date, but what if she says no?

Our feelings can be either our best friend or our worst enemy, depending on the action (or inaction) that we take.

Knowing what to do AND knowing why you want to do it won't ever be enough. So what's the solution?

In Mel Robbins's words, "If you have an impulse to act on a goal, you must physically move within 5 seconds or your brain will kill the idea." Start the countdown once you get the impulse, and then take ACTION!

What does this look like in real life?

When you see that person you've been wanting to meet, you start the countdown:

5....4....3....2....1 say hi and introduce yourself!

When your boss asks if anyone has any ideas for the upcoming project, you start the countdown:

5....4....3....2....1 speak up!

There are hundreds and hundreds of opportunities each day that you can use the 5-Second Rule to overcome your shyness and become a more effective communicator.

Ralph Waldo Emerson is quoted as saying, "Do the thing and you will have the power. But they that do not the thing, have not the power."

No more pondering and contemplating the life you want to live and the person you want to become! The POWER and magic starts to happen when we go for it.

No matter how many books we read, audios we listen to, seminars we attend, nothing changes until we DO the thing. If we wait until we have the courage or motivation, we'll be waiting the rest of our lives.

If you let it, this secret sauce can transform your entire life because it's grounded in TAKING ACTION!

My Twist on the 5-Second Rule

When I first learned about Mel Robbins' simple yet incredible effective strategy, I saw immediate results.

I *finally* was able to stay consistent with my 4:00 wake-up call, and every morning (to this day) when it's time to jump into a cold shower, I begin my countdown.

When I'm out running errands and feel the urge to share a compliment or ask a question to a stranger, I begin the countdown.

When I need to make call for our business that I'd been avoiding, I begin the countdown.

However, I did make a slight adjustment to it.

I noticed that five seconds was a little too much time to give my brain before it went back to panic mode and I talked myself out of it. I decided to cut the time down to 3 seconds, and it worked like a charm.

I'm not going to sit here and pretend that I'm perfect with this technique (or any of those that I've given to you). I still let my fear get the best of me at times, and I hold back. But I don't beat myself up about it anymore because I know that this is a lifetime commitment to improvement (which we'll talk about in the next chapter).

Right here, *right now*, think about something you've been wanting to do for a while now but keep putting off. It doesn't need to be a grand gesture like giving a speech or anything like that. It can literally be as simple as making plans with a friend, telling someone "I'm sorry," or even cleaning your room.

Once you've locked in what you need to do, put down this book, and start the countdown:

5....4....3....2....1 GO!

(You can even make it a 3-second countdown.)

If you start to doubt yourself with *Yeah, but...* then start the countdown over again!

Don't wait another minute. Do it now and start practicing this (especially in social situations) as much as possible.

This technique will help you see INSTANT progress in your conversation skills, but remember that this is a....

Chapter 12:

LIFETIME COMMITMENT TO GROWTH

Did you try out the 5-Second Rule from last chapter? How did it go? How do you feel?

If not, put the book down now and go do it right now!

Let me remind you the purpose of this book is to start taking action so you can make the changes to become more of your *True Self*.

Assuming you've done it and started using the other *Back Pocket Tips* in your daily life, we can move forward, as this journey together is coming to an end...for now.

There Is No Finish Line

Since reading *Control the Crazy* for the first time, I've gone back and re-read that book multiple times. I needed that constant reminder of ideas and strategies that would help me detach from believing in the negative thoughts that would creep into my consciousness.

I believed in that book so much that I started sharing it with anyone who was interested and gave them my Kindle information so that they could log into my account and read the book for free.

I gave it to so many people that I eventually was locked out of my account and couldn't download it because too many devices had used my login. I took this as a sign to start searching for other books with similar ideas.

Since then, I've read over 200 books (and thousands of hours of audio) in the areas of psychology, sociology, and human development. Amazon puts many of these books in the genre of Self-Help but I like to think of it as Self-Discovery.

I'm sharing this not to brag or boost my ego, but to encourage you to commit to a lifetime of discovering yourself through books and audios that can change your mindset and, ultimately, your life.

I like to think of the ideas from the books and audios being seeds planted in my brain. Growth occurs when I take action on the ideas from the book. Action is like rain and sunshine; without it, seeds won't sprout and grow. I never know when the harvest will come, but when it does, it feels amazing.

I hope you go back and read this book again and share it with your friends, but I'm also hopeful that you will seek out other authors, speakers, and people who have the skills, knowledge, and insight that you wish to develop.

Albert Einstein said, "Once you stop learning, you start dying."

The irony is that I used to hate reading. I was an average student and got through school by skimming through books or looking them up on SparkNotes.

My self-esteem, confidence, and inner-peace started to increase once I realized that learning isn't about memorizing facts but is, instead, a journey of becoming aware of ourselves and strengthening our minds.

The Next Step

My invitation to you is simple. I'm asking you to commit to a lifetime of personal development so that you can become the best version of yourself that you can be. In other words, your *True Self.*

I want you to start envisioning your life once you've overcome your shyness. Who do you want to be? What do you want to do? Where do you want to go? What kind of legacy do you want to leave behind for your family and the world around you?

If we're only focused on overcoming shyness, we're vulnerable to remaining stuck in that illusion for longer than we'd like.

We only have one shot at this thing called life, my friend, and even if you believe in reincarnation, isn't it about time you get off the wheel of birth, mediocre life, and death? I'm **certain** that you have talents, abilities, and gifts that the world needs to witness. I'm giving you permission to be yourself in a world that tries to label and define you as you're "supposed" to be.

Don't give in. Be bold and unapologetically YOU in your pursuit and commitment to live a life that you can be proud of.

I believe in you.

5...4...3...2...1 You got this!

BONUS:

THE BEST ADVICE I'VE EVER RECEIVED

You've got all you need to overcome shyness, break out of your shell, and express more of your True Self! And when you don't *feel* like doing it, you now know to start counting down (from 5 or 3) and TAKE ACTION!

As we conclude our journey together with this book, I want to share one last story with you. It's the message that has forever changed my life and I know it can do the same for you.

My dad and I started a morning tradition on my first day of middle school that lasted until my junior year of high school.

Every morning, he would drive me to school and it was our 10 minutes to talk about sports, school, girls, and life. Despite any drama and chaos that was going on at home (and there was a lot of it), this was our place of peace together.

I could talk to my dad about anything and felt safe that he wasn't going to judge or criticize me. He played his father role but also felt like a best friend.

Once we pulled up to school, he would turn towards me, give me a few bucks for lunch followed by a big hug, and he'd always say, "Be the best you can be today, Buddy!"

As a teenager, that was a nice little saying but I didn't yet comprehend the depth and true meaning of it.

Years have gone by and life's challenges and obstacles have presented themselves in various forms. I've come to really cherish those moments we had together each morning and develop a greater appreciation for those seven words that he instilled in me.

To be the best we can be, we must become self-aware, practice gratitude daily, live in a beautiful state of mind, be honest with ourselves and others, admit our mistakes, remain humble, love unconditionally, seek adventure, commit to growth, live outside of our comfort zones, and (maybe most importantly) contribute to making other people's lives better.

Thank you for letting me be part of your journey, and I'm hopeful that at least one idea from this book can make a profound impact on your life so that you can better serve those people around you.

Be the best YOU can be today and every day moving forward!

Your friend,
Erik Myers

INVITATION: You're Not Alone

One of the biggest lies I repeated to myself over and over again when my shyness was holding me back from being true to myself was that no one else could possibly understand how I was feeling. I felt isolated from the world around me because I unconsciously **chose** to disconnect.

It wasn't until I began to open up that I discovered that so many others felt the same way I did. We all have different experiences, but our feelings are universal.

There were so many people and communities that believed in me before I could believe in myself, and I now feel responsible to create a safe online community where people can connect, share stories, be inspired, celebrate small wins, trade tips and techniques, and ultimately support each other.

Our community is already growing faster than I expected and the only thing we're missing is...YOU!

To join the Facebook group, simply go to www.facebook.com/groups/overcomingshyness and request to join. There you'll be able to meet people who have felt what you feel and you will make new friends along the journey.

I'll be posting videos, quotes, or articles daily and encourage you to contribute to the group. I'm excited to see you in there!

If we aren't yet connected on social media, I'd love to follow you and your journey! Follow me on Instagram (@erikmyers4) and www.facebook.com/erikmyers4. Don't hesitate to send me a direct message, leave a comment, or ask a question! I do my best to respond daily. Talk to you soon!

BOOK ERIK TO SPEAK!

Book Erik to speak at your event or school and he's guaranteed to deliver an inspiring, heartfelt, and captivating experience for everyone in attendance!

For more info – Email Erik@overcomingshyness.co

Thank you for reading my book!

I really appreciate all of your feedback and I love hearing your thoughts.

I need your input to make the next version of this book and my future books better.

Please take 1-2 minutes to leave me a helpful review on Amazon and let me know what you thought of the book!

Thank you so much!

Your friend,
Erik Myers

THANK YOU to my amazing
Launch Team members!

Alex Levy
Allie Hirschi
Alyna Zain Joosab
Anissa L. Jackson
Ashley Clouthier
Batool Yogima
Ben Schingen
Beverly Adamo
Bryan Cargill
Cardo Morin
Cassandra Garcia
Charvee Pandya
Cynthia Hernandez
David Pollock
Derek Denz
Dominique Myers
Elenah Kangara
Gemma Willsher
Hoku Laanui
Innocent Magongoa
Jacquelyn Elnor Johnson
James Irvine
Jasmine Renae
Jason Troxel
Jerry Ratigan
Jing Hua
John Gehrke
K.L. Dimago
Kamve'Lihle Nkohla
Katy Bothwell
Kayla Cupit

Keisa Fruge
Kevin Jacobson
Kristina Schoenhals
Anderson
Lore Mendez
Marko Pfann
Marla Lively
Matthew Langley
Michael Lee Lacey
Michele Laine
Nicole Tracy
Ray Brehm
Rebecca Tervo
Sabrina Zainal
Sam Temporal
Sarah Olson
Shannon Marie
Shola Kaye
Sofiane Dri
Subhanah Wahhaj
Tanis Melanie Jaarsma
Tessa Bechmann
Tia Lidstrom
Couad Lengliz
Jennifer Walters
Ndeye Labadens
Alan McComas
Jessie Risk Sutton
Sue Wilson
Habiba Raffa